USBORNE

THE GREAT DINOSAUR SEARCH

Rosie Heywood

Illustrated by Studio Galante and Inklink Firenze

Edited by Philippa Wingate

Managing designer: Mary Cartwright

Scientific consultant: Dr. David Norman

Contents

About this book

This is a book all about dinosaurs and the world they lived in. It's also an exciting puzzle book. If you look hard at the pictures, you'll be able to spot hundreds of dinosaurs and the creatures that lived at the same time as them. You can see below how the puzzles work.

The writing next to each little picture tells you the name of the animal or plant and how many you can find in the big picture.

Look very carefully to count all the dinosaurs in the distance.

This Protoceratops is hatching, but it still counts.

These young dinosaurs also count.

Although this lizard is coming out of the big picture, you should still count it.

You can only see part of this Protoceratops, but it still counts.

There are about 100 animals to spot in each picture. If you get stuck, the answers are on pages 28–31. Not all the animals are dinosaurs, only the ones with a symbol next to them like the one on the right. In real life there wouldn't have been this many animals in one place at the same time.

Dinosaur symbol

Shallow seas

Over 400 million years ago, the Silurian seas were full of strange creatures. Many of these have died out, but some, such as sponges and jellyfish, can still be found in the oceans today.

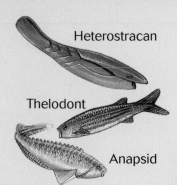

Heterostracan

Thelodont

Anapsid

These fish sucked food and water through their mouths. Find seven of each type.

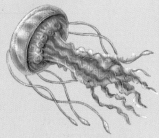

Jellyfish looked much the same as they do now. Spot five.

Brachiopods were animals with fleshy stalks which they buried in the sand. Find 14.

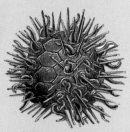

Sea urchins crawled slowly across the sea floor. Spot eight.

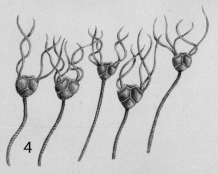

Sea-lilies were animals, not plants. They caught food with their wavy arms. Spot 15.

Marine snails could hide inside their shells. Find 14.

Nostolepis was one of the first fish to have jaws and teeth. Spot 13.

Osteostracan fish had bony shields covering their heads. Spot nine.

Cephalopods were decorated with beautiful patterns. Spot four of each of these.

Silurian starfish didn't look the same as modern starfish. Spot 11.

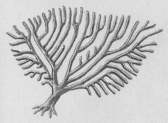

Graptolites were made up of lots of small animals joined together. Find two.

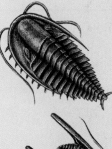

Shrimps like the one above darted through the shallow water. Find 14.

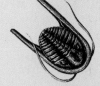

Trilobites walked along the sea floor, looking for food. Spot 12.

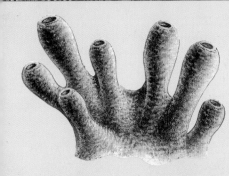

Sponges were animals with soft, fleshy bodies. Spot five.

This giant Eurypterid was a fierce hunter. Can you spot another one?

Living on the land

400 million years ago, fish with lungs for breathing air began to crawl out of the water. These fish slowly changed over millions of years, until they had legs for walking and could live on land.

Bothriolepis used its jointed fins to walk along the bottom of lakes. Spot five.

Clubmosses had branching stems covered with tiny, scaly leaves. Find nine plants.

Scientists think Aglaophyton was one of the first plants to grow on land. Spot six.

These are Ichthyostega eggs. Spot four groups.

Ichthyostega could walk on land, but it also had a fish-like tail. Spot four.

Groenlandaspis was a fish with bony plates to protect its head. Find five.

Shark-like Ctenacanthus glided through the water in search of prey. Spot one.

Ichthyostegopsis used its flipper-like legs to swim after fish. Find two.

Panderichthys had four fins that looked like arms and legs. Can you find three?

You can still see horsetail plants in wet and marshy places. Spot 16.

Water beetles looked the same as they do today. Find nine.

These woodlice were one of the first animals to live on land. Spot ten.

Shrimps fed on tiny bits of food which floated in the water. Can you find 15?

Acanthostega had gills like a fish, for breathing underwater. Spot seven.

Mimia fishes were about the size of your thumb. Spot 18.

Eusthenopteron used its fins to prop itself up on the banks of lakes and rivers. Spot three.

Giant insects

In the steamy Carboniferous swamps, gigantic insects zoomed through the air, while venomous bugs crawled through the thick, tangled undergrowth.

Pholidogaster was a strong swimmer and a fierce hunter. Spot two.

Meganeura had a wingspan that was as long as a human's arm. Spot four.

Cockroaches had flat bodies. They could squeeze under things to hide. Spot 15.

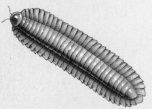

The centipede Arthropleura sometimes grew up to 2m (6½ft) long. Find six.

The word Hylonomus means "forest mouse". Spot seven.

Gephyrostegus had sharp teeth for crunching up insects. Spot six.

Giant scorpions could kill other animals by stinging them. Find three.

8

Archaeothyris had strong jaws which helped it to kill its prey. Find three.

The first snails appeared on land at this time. Before, they had lived underwater. Spot ten.

Lizard-like microsaurs lived on land but laid their eggs in water. Spot 11.

Ophiderpeton had no arms or legs, and looked like an eel. Can you spot five?

Spiders spun simple webs to catch their prey. Find seven.

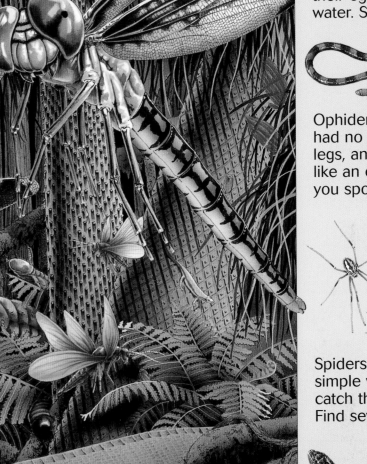

Westlothiana was a reptile. It laid eggs with hard shells and lived on dry land. Spot ten.

Giant millipedes fed on rotting leaves. Spot five.

Eogyrinus was the size of a crocodile. It snapped up fish in its powerful jaws. Find four.

Gerrothorax lay at the bottom of rivers, waiting to catch passing fish. Spot one.

9

Rocky landscape

During this time, lots of animals appeared that could live on land. The most striking of these had huge sails on their backs. Many of these creatures died out before the arrival of the dinosaurs.

Yougina had strong, sharp teeth for cracking open snail shells. Spot three.

Pareiasaurus grew as big as a hippopotamus. Spot three.

Protorosaurus reared up on its back legs to catch insects to eat. Find four.

Sphenacodon had a ridge on its back. Spot six.

Seymouria couldn't move fast on land. It spent most of its time in water. Spot three.

Scientists know Sauroctonus was a meat-eater, because its teeth were long and sharp. Find four.

Diadectes had legs which stuck out on either side of its body, just like a modern lizard. Spot seven.

Edaphosaurus warmed itself up by letting the Sun heat the blood in a sail on its back. Can you spot 11?

Moschops was the size of a cow. Can you find four?

Cacops had a big head compared to the size of its body. Spot nine.

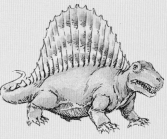

Long bones sticking out from Dimetrodon's spine held up a sail on its back. Find five.

Eryops was a distant relative of modern frogs. Spot two.

Anteosaurus bit chunks of flesh off its prey, then swallowed them whole. Spot two.

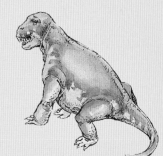

Casea had teeth all over the roof of its mouth, to crush up plants. Find four.

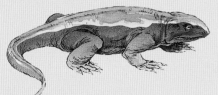

Scutosaurus had thick skin, and spikes sticking out of its cheeks. Spot three.

Bradysaurus had a neck frill at the back of its skull. Find one.

The first dinosaurs

About 225 million years ago, the first dinosaurs appeared. There are six different kinds of dinosaurs to spot here, along with some of the other strange creatures that lived at the same time.

Kuehneosaurus had thin sails of skin, which it used to glide from tree to tree. Spot four.

Although Cynognathus looked a little like a dog, it had scaly skin. Spot one.

Terrestrisuchus was about the size of a squirrel. Spot eight.

The dinosaur Staurikosaurus probably hunted in packs. Can you find seven?

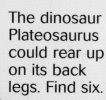

The dinosaur Plateosaurus could rear up on its back legs. Find six.

Rutiodon had nostrils on the top of its head, between its eyes. Find two.

Ticinosuchus had strong, long legs so it could move very quickly. Spot five.

Saltopus, a dinosaur, scampered over rocks searching for lizards to eat. Can you find ten?

Syntarsus had sharp eyes and great speed to help it catch its prey. Spot four.

Peteinosaurus was one of the first flying lizards. Find three.

Placerias lived in herds and roamed long distances in search of food. Spot ten.

Desmatosuchus had long spikes sticking out from its shoulders. Spot three.

The dinosaur Coelophysis was a skilful hunter. Find seven.

Anchisaurus was one of the first dinosaurs. It was 2.5m (8ft) long. Spot five.

Stagonolepis may have dug for roots with its snout. Can you spot four?

Thrinaxodon had whiskers on its face and a furry body. Find five.

In the forest

The largest dinosaurs ever to walk the Earth lived at this time. Growing to enormous sizes, these giant creatures fed on the lush trees and plants which grew in the warm, wet climate.

Brachiosaurus' nostrils were on the top of a bump on its head. Spot one.

Pterodactylus snapped insects out of the air as it flew. Spot ten.

Apatosaurus swallowed leaves whole because it could not chew. Spot five.

Camptosaurus could run on its back legs if it was chased. Find two.

Fierce meat-eater Ceratosaurus had over 70 saw-edged fangs. Spot one.

Compsognathus is one of the smallest known dinosaurs. It was no bigger than a cat. Find eight.

Camarasaurus ate leaves from the lower tree branches. Spot three.

Diplodocus was as long as three buses parked end to end. Can you spot six?

Dryosaurus may have lived in herds like modern deer. Spot 17.

Archaeopteryx was probably the first bird. It flew from tree to tree. Find three.

Kentrosaurus had large spines on its back and tail. Spot one.

Scaphognathus had excellent eyesight. Can you find two?

Allosaurus had bony ridges above its eyes. Spot three.

Ornitholestes used its sharp claws to grab lizards and other small animals. Spot three.

Coelurus had long legs and could run fast to catch its prey. Spot two.

The bony plates on Stegosaurus' back may have absorbed heat from the Sun. Find two.

In the ocean

While dinosaurs roamed the land in Jurassic times, huge reptiles swam through the vast oceans.

There are 87 creatures to spot on these two pages. How many can you find?

Pleurosaurus had a long body and an even longer tail. Can you spot four?

Brittle stars still live in today's oceans. They have five long arms. Spot eight.

Plesiosaurus flapped its fins slowly up and down like a turtle. Find two.

Sharks sank to the bottom of the ocean if they didn't keep swimming. Spot six.

Liopleurodon ate other large sea creatures such as ichthyosaurs. Spot one.

Pleurosternon needed to go up to the surface to breathe. Can you spot two?

Rhomaleosaurus was as big as a modern killer whale, and just as fierce. Spot two.

King crabs walked along the ocean floor. Spot three.

Belemnites had suckers on their arms. Spot ten.

Ichthyosaurus could swim fast by moving its powerful tail. Spot four.

Crocodile-like Geosaurus had paddle-shaped flippers. Find two.

Eurhinosaurus had a very long top jaw with lots of sharp teeth. Spot three.

Ammonites used their long tentacles to catch food. Find 14.

Banjo fish used their wing-like fins to glide through the water. Spot five.

There were many different kinds of fish. Spot ten of each of these.

Teleosaurus swam with snake-like movements. Spot one.

17

Dusty desert

The dinosaurs that lived in desert areas of what is now Mongolia and China suffered terrible dust storms. Some choked to death, while others were buried alive in sand dunes.

Oviraptor built nests for its eggs and sat on them until they hatched. Spot 12.

Psittacosaurus had a bony beak like a parrot's. Find four adults and six young.

Tarbosaurus ran after its prey with powerful bursts of speed. Can you find one?

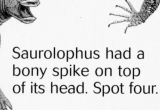

Saurolophus had a bony spike on top of its head. Spot four.

These lizards fed on dinosaur eggs. Find eight.

If Pinacosaurus was attacked, it used the club on its tail as a weapon. Spot two.

Protoceratops laid its eggs in nests in the sand. Find five.

Protoceratops' nest

Microceratops was about the size of a rabbit. Spot 15.

Saurornithoides had large eyes and may have been able to see in the dark. Find ten.

Small mammals ran through the undergrowth catching insects to eat. Spot five.

Bactrosaurus had hundreds of teeth for chewing tough leaves. Spot seven.

Velociraptor means "speedy killer". It was a vicious meat-eater. Spot six.

Gallimimus ran on its back legs like an ostrich, but it didn't have any feathers. Find 11.

Avimimus was unusual, because it had feathers on its body. Spot seven.

Homalocephale had a thick skull with knobs on the sides. Spot three.

19

The last dinosaurs

During the late Cretaceous Period, there were more types of dinosaurs than at any other point in history. But then, about 64 million years ago, the dinosaurs suddenly died out.

Parasaurolophus used a tube on its head to make trumpet-like noises. Spot six.

Styracosaurus looked very fierce, but it only ate plants. Can you spot one?

Corythosaurus had a crest-like helmet on its head. Spot three.

Edmontosaurus lived in groups for protection against predators. Spot eight.

Panoplosaurus had spikes on its sides, but its belly was unprotected. Find two.

Pachycephalosaurus males had head-butting contests. Can you find five?

Triceratops weighed twice as much as an elephant. Spot four adults and two young.

20

Euoplocephalus may have swung the club on the end of its tail at attackers. Find three.

Ferocious hunter Tyrannosaurus was taller than a modern giraffe. Spot one.

Stenonychosaurus may have been clever, because it had a big brain. Find seven.

Ichthyornis was one of the first birds. Find six.

Struthiomimus looked like an ostrich, but with no feathers. Spot nine.

Stegoceras belonged to a group of dinosaurs called dome heads. Spot seven.

Pentaceratops had a neck frill which reached halfway down its back. Spot three.

Nodosaurus means "lumpy reptile". Spot two.

Dromaeosaurus killed larger dinosaurs by hunting in packs. Spot 12.

Woodland mammals

When the dinosaurs died out, mammals took their place. Mammals are warm-blooded animals. They have fur or hair, give birth to babies and feed them with milk.

Tetonis gripped onto branches with its strong hands and feet. Spot five.

These bats hunted insects at night and slept during the day. Spot five.

Hyrachus was about the size of a pig. It could run very fast. Spot six.

Uintatherium was as large as a rhino, with six bony lumps on its head. Spot one.

Smilodectes used its long tail for balance as it climbed trees. Spot four.

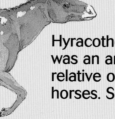

Hyracotherium was an ancient relative of horses. Spot 11.

Coryphodon means "curved tusks". It may have used them to defend itself. Spot three.

Mesonyx had teeth like a dog, but hooves instead of paws. Find three.

Diatryma was a giant bird. It stood 2m (6½ft) tall. Spot two.

Notharctus looked a little like a monkey. Spot seven.

Leptictidium was an omnivore, which means it ate plants and animals. Spot eight.

Oxyaena was a cat-like hunter that crept up on its prey. Spot two.

Venomous snakes curled around branches to sleep. Spot three.

Moeritherium probably lived in and around water. Spot one.

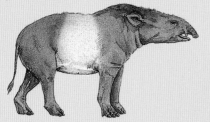

Eomanis had no teeth. It used its long tongue to lick up ants. Spot two.

Archaeotherium used its strong sense of smell to sniff out tasty roots. Spot ten.

The Ice ages

During the Ice ages, the climate switched between very warm and extremely cold, with thick snow and ice. Here you can see some of the animals that lived in these different climates.

Columbian mammoths had tusks over 4m (13ft) long. Spot four.

Long-horned bison had poor eyesight. Can you find 12?

Woolly rhinos pushed away the snow with their horns to reach grass. Spot one.

Male cave lions were larger than lions today, but they didn't have manes. Spot one.

Like modern camels, Western camels stored water in their humps. Can you spot two?

Dire wolves used their strong teeth to crush up bones. Find six.

Ground sloths had bony lumps under their skin for protection. Spot one.

Teratornis swooped down to feed on dead animals. Can you find two?

Cave bears went into caves to sleep through the coldest weather. Spot two.

Grey wolves lived and hunted in packs of up to ten animals. Find seven.

Arctic hares had white fur so wolves couldn't see them against the snow. Spot seven.

Herds of ancient bison roamed the plains in search of food. Spot nine.

Reindeer had wide feet to stop them from sinking into the snow. Find ten.

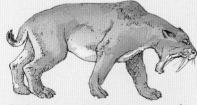
Sabre-toothed cats used their huge fangs to kill other animals. Spot two.

Woolly mammoths had very thick, shaggy fur to keep them warm. Find four.

Western horses died out 10,000 years ago, but no one knows why. Find 12.

25

Death of the dinosaurs

About 64 million years ago, almost all the dinosaurs died out. No one is certain why. Most scientists believe that an enormous meteorite (a rock from space) may have hit the Earth. It may have measured as much as 10km (6 miles) across.

Clouds of dust

When the meteorite hit the Earth, it would have caused a huge ball of fire to spread around the world. The meteorite would have smashed into tiny pieces, surrounding the planet with clouds of dust, rocks and water. The cloud would have blocked out all the Sun's light, making the Earth cold and dark for months.

This picture shows what may have happened as the meteorite struck the Earth.

Huge clouds of dust spread out over the Earth, making it hard for animals to breathe.

Animals dying

This would have killed any creatures that needed warmth to survive. Without light, many plants must have died as well, leaving many of the dinosaurs with nothing to eat. The meteorite may also have caused massive earthquakes and huge tidal waves.

Dinosaurs were killed or injured by pieces of flying rock.

Dinosaur puzzle

These dinosaurs are ones that you've seen already in the book. How much can you remember about them?

You may need to look back to help you with this puzzle. If you get really stuck, you'll find the answers on page 28.

1. Only one of these animals had an unusual covering of feathers on its body. Which one was it?

A   B   C   D   E

2. Can you guess which of these creatures was the first bird?

A   B   C   D   E

3. Which of these could kill another animal by stinging it?

A   B   C   D   E

4. Four of these are animals, and only one is a plant. Can you guess which one it is?

A   B   C   D   E

5. Which one of these dinosaurs did not eat meat?

A   B   C   D   E

6. Which of these fish could use its jointed fins to walk along the bottom of a lake?

A   B   C   D   E

Answers

The keys on pages 28 to 31 show you where all the animals and plants you have been asked to spot appear on the pictures in this book. Use the keys if you get stuck trying to find a particular animal or plant.

Answers to the dinosaur puzzle on page 27:

1. C
2. E
3. A
4. A
5. C
6. B

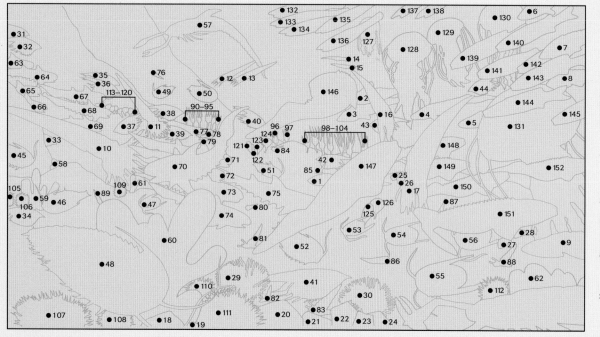

Shallow seas 4–5

Osteostracan fish
 1 2 3 4 5 6 7 8 9

Cephalopods 10 11
 12 13 14 15 16 17

Starfish 18 19 20 21
 22 23 24 25 26
 27 28

Graptolites 29 30

Shrimps 31 32 33
 34 35 36 37 38
 39 40 41 42 43
 44

Trilobites 45 46 47
 48 49 50 51 52
 53 54 55 56

Eurypterid 57

Sponges 58 59 60
 61 62

Nostolepis 63 64 65
 66 67 68 69 70
 71 72 73 74 75

Marine snails 76 77
 78 79 80 81 82
 83 84 85 86 87
 88 89

Sea-lilies 90 91 92
 93 94 95 96 97
 98 99 100 101
 102 103 104

Sea urchins 105
 106 107 108 109
 110 111 112

Brachiopods 113 114
 115 116 117 118
 119 120 121 122
 123 124 125 126

Jellyfish 127 128 129
 130 131

Heterostracan 132
 133 134 135 136
 137 138

Thelodont 139 140
 141 142 143 144
 145

Anapsid 146 147 148
 149 150 151 152

Living on the land 6–7

Ichthyostegopsis 1 2

Panderichthys 3 4 5

Horsetail plants 6 7
 8 9 10 11 12 13 14
 15 16 17 18 19
 20 21

Water beetles 22 23
 24 25 26 27 28
 29 30

Woodlice 31 32 33
 34 35 36 37 38
 39 40

Shrimps 41 42 43
 44 45 46 47 48
 49 50 51 52 53
 54 55

Eusthenopteron 56
 57 58

Mimia 59 60 61 62
 63 64 65 66 67
 68 69 70 71 72
 73 74 75 76

Acanthostega 77 78
 79 80 81 82 83

Ctenacanthus 84

Groenlandaspis 85
 86 87 88 89

Ichthyostega 90 91
 92 93

Ichthyostega's eggs
 94 95 96 97

Aglaophyton 98 99
 100 101 102 103

Clubmosses 104
 105 106 107 108
 109 110 111 112

Bothriolepis 113 114
 115 116 117

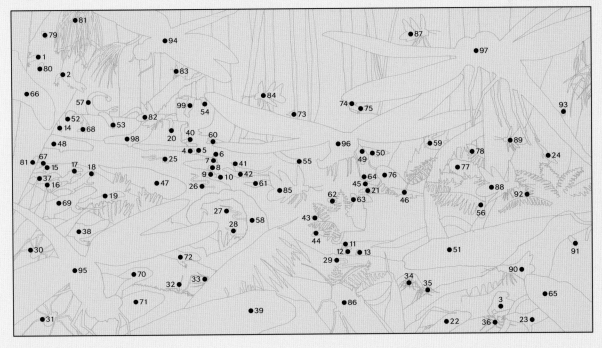

Giant insects 8−9

Archaeothyris 1 2 3
Land snails 4 5 6 7
8 9 10 11 12 13
Microsaurs 14 15 16
17 18 19 20 21
22 23 24
Ophiderpeton 25 26
27 28 29
Spiders 30 31 32
33 34 35 36
Westlothiana 37 38
39 40 41 42 43
44 45 46
Gerrothorax 47
Eogyrinus 48 49 50
51
Giant millipedes 52
53 54 55 56
Giant scorpions 57
58 59
Gephyrostegus 60
61 62 63 64 65
Hylonomus 66 67
68 69 70 71 72
Arthropleura 73 74
75 76 77 78

Cockroaches 79 80
81 82 83 84 85
86 87 88 89 90
91 92 93
Meganeura 94 95
96 97
Pholidogaster 98 99

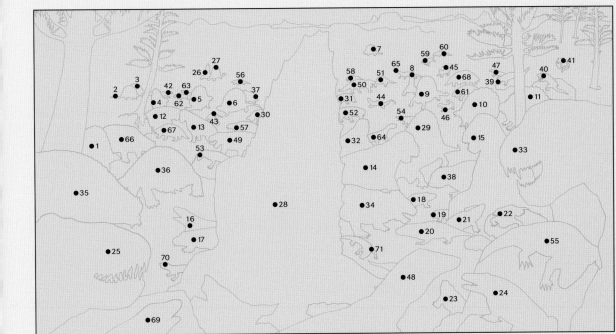

Rocky landscape 10−11

Edaphosaurus 1 2 3
4 5 6 7 8 9 10 11
Moschops 12 13 14
15
Cacops 16 17 18 19
20 21 22 23 24
Dimetrodon 25 26
27 28 29
Eryops 30 31
Anteosaurus 32 33
Bradysaurus 34
Scutosaurus 35 36
37
Casea 38 39 40 41
Diadectes 42 43 44
45 46 47 48
Sauroctonus 49 50
51 52 .
Seymouria 53 54 55
Sphenacodon 56 57
58 59 60 61
Protorosaurus 62 63
64 65
Pareiasaurus 66 67
68
Yougina 69 70 71

The first dinosaurs 12−13

Saltopus 1 2 3 4 5 6
7 8 9 10
Syntarsus 11 12 13
14
Peteinosaurus 15 16
17
Placerias 18 19 20
21 22 23 24 25
26 27
Desmatosuchus 28
29 30
Coelophysis 31 32
33 34 35 36 37
Thrinaxodon 38 39
40 41 42
Stagonolepis 43 44
45 46
Anchisaurus 47 48
49 50 51
Ticinosuchus 52 53
54 55 56
Rutiodon 57 58
Plateosaurus 59 60
61 62 63 64
Staurikosaurus 65
66 67 68 69 70
71

Terrestrisuchus 72
73 74 75 76 77
78 79
Cynognathus 80
Kuehneosaurus 81
82 83 84

29

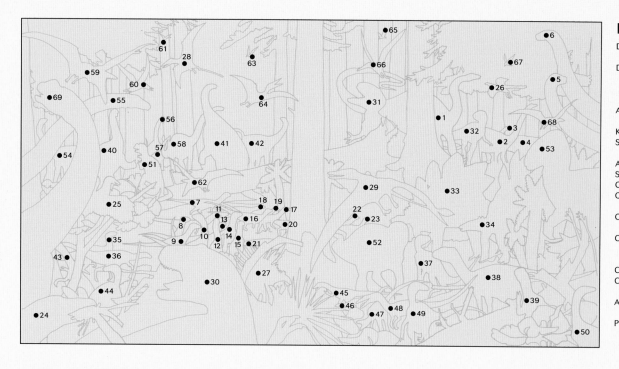

In the forest 14–15

Diplodocus 1 2 3 4
5 6
Dryosaurus 7 8 9 10
11 12 13 14 15 16
17 18 19 20 21
22 23
Archaeopteryx 24
25 26
Kentrosaurus 27
Scaphognathus 28
29
Allosaurus 30 31 32
Stegosaurus 33 34
Coelurus 35 36
Ornitholestes 37 38
39
Camarasaurus 40 41
42
Compsognathus 43
44 45 46 47 48
49 50
Ceratosaurus 51
Camptosaurus 52
53
Apatosaurus 54 55
56 57 58
Pterodactylus 59 60
61 62 63 64 65
66 67 68

Brachiosaurus 69

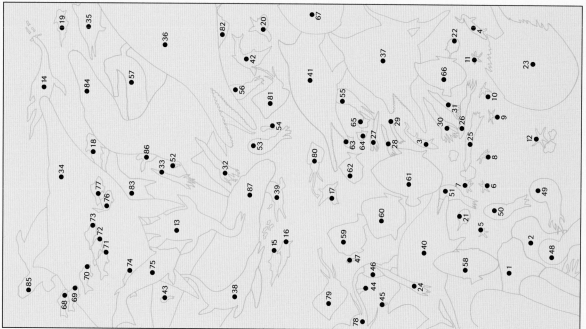

In the ocean 16–17

Pleurosaurus 1 2 3 4
Brittle stars 5 6 7 8
9 10 11 12
Plesiosaurus 13 14
Sharks 15 16 17 18
19 20
King crabs 21 22 23
Belemnites 24 25
26 27 28 29 30
31 32 33
Ichthyosaurus 34
35 36 37
Geosaurus 38 39
Eurhinosaurus 40 41
42
Ammonites 43 44
45 46 47 48 49
50 51 52 53 54
55 56
Teleosaurus 57
Fish 58 59 60 61
62 63 64 65 66
67 68 69 70 71
72 73 74 75 76
77
Banjo fish 78 79 80
81 82
Rhomaleosaurus 83
84

Pleurosternon 85 86
Liopleurodon 87

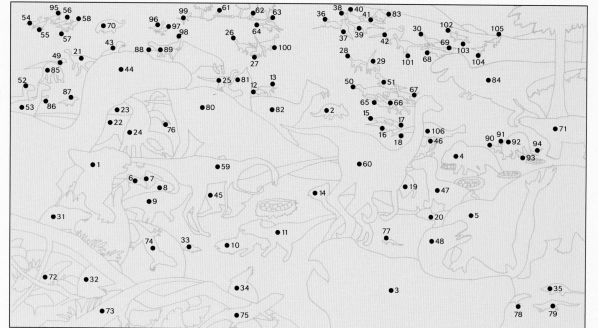

Dusty desert 18–19

Protoceratops 1 2 3
4 5
Microceratops 6 7
8 9 10 11 12 13 14
15 16 17 18 19
20
Saurornithoides 21
22 23 24 25 26
27 28 29 30
Mammals 31 32 33
34 35
Bactrosaurus 36 37
38 39 40 41 42
Velociraptor 43 44
45 46 47 48
Homalocephale 49
50 51
Avimimus 52 53 54
55 56 57 58
Gallimimus 59 60
61 62 63 64 65
66 67 68 69
Pinacosaurus 70 71
Lizards 72 73 74 75
76 77 78 79
Saurolophus 80 81
82 83
Tarbosaurus 84

Psittacosaurus 85 86
87 88 89 90 91
92 93 94
Oviraptor 95 96 97
98 99 100 101
102 103 104 105
106

30

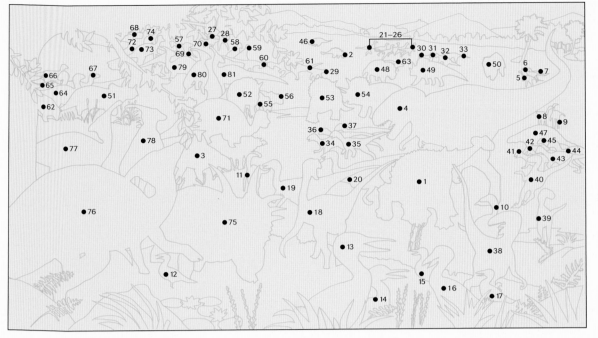

The last dinosaurs 20–21

Euoplocephalus 1 2
3
Tyrannosaurus 4
Stenonychosaurus 5
6 7 8 9 10 11
Ichthyornis 12 13 14
15 16 17
Struthiomimus 18 19
20 21 22 23 24
25 26
Stegoceras 27 28
29 30 31 32 33
Dromaeosaurus 34
35 36 37 38 39
40 41 42 43 44
45
Nodosaurus 46 47
Pentaceratops 48 49
50
Triceratops 51 52 53
54 55 56
Pachycephalosaurus
57 58 59 60 61
Panoplosaurus 62
63
Edmontosaurus 64
65 66 67 68 69
70 71

Corythosaurus 72
73 74
Styracosaurus 75
Parasaurolophus 76
77 78 79 80 81

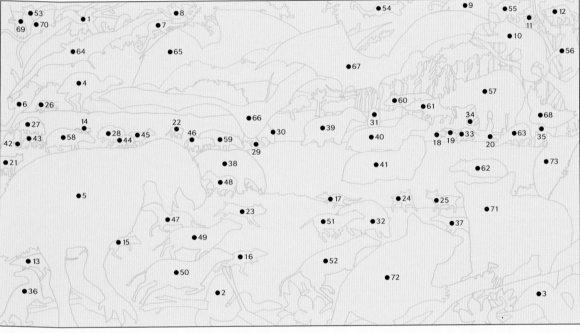

Woodland mammals 22–23

Snakes 1 2 3
Diatryma 4 5
Notharctus 6 7 8 9
10 11 12
Leptictidium 13 14
15 16 17 18 19 20
Oxyaena 21 22
Mesonyx 23 24 25
Archaeotherium 26
27 28 29 30 31
32 33 34 35
Eomanis 36 37
Moeritherium 38
Coryphodon 39 40
41
Hyracotherium 42
43 44 45 46 47
48 49 50 51 52
Smilodectes 53 54
55 56
Uintatherium 57
Hyrachus 58 59 60
61 62 63
Bats 64 65 66 67
68
Tetonis 69 70 71 72
73

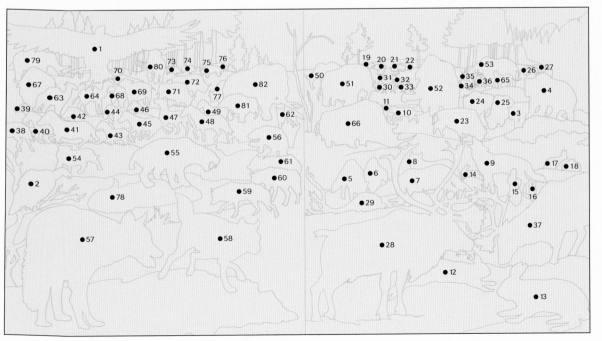

The Ice ages 24–25

Teratornis 1 2
Cave bears 3 4
Grey wolves 5 6 7 8
9 10 11
Arctic hares 12 13 14
15 16 17 18
Ancient bison 19 20
21 22 23 24 25
26 27
Reindeer 28 29 30
31 32 33 34 35
36 37
Western horses 38
39 40 41 42 43
44 45 46 47 48
49
Woolly mammoths
50 51 52 53
Sabre-toothed cats
54 55
Ground sloth 56
Dire wolves 57 58
59 60 61 62
Western camels 63
64
Cave lion 65
Woolly rhino 66

Long-horned bison
67 68 69 70 71
72 73 74 75 76
77 78
Columbian
mammoths 79 80
81 82

31

Index

Cover and additional design by Stephanie Jones • Additional editing by Claire Masset
With thanks to John Russell, Natalie Abi-Ezzi, Rebecca Mills and Katarina Dragoslavić